From Your Friends At **The M**

M000114833

APRIL

A MONTH OF REPRODUCIBLES AT YOUR FINGERTIPS!

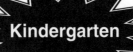

Kindergarten

Editor:
Angie Kutzer

Writers:
Susan Bunyan, Susan DeRiso, Rhonda Dominguez,
Diane Gilliam, Lucia Kemp Henry, Angie Kutzer

Art Coordinator:
Clevell Harris

Artists:
Susan Bunyan, Nick Greenwood, Clevell Harris,
Lucia Kemp Henry, Susan Hodnett, Sheila Krill,
Rob Mayworth, Kimberly Richard,
Rebecca Saunders, Donna K. Teal

Cover Artist:
Jennifer Tipton Bennett

www.themailbox.com

©1998 by THE EDUCATION CENTER, INC.
All rights reserved.
ISBN #1-56234-228-2

Manufactured in the United States

10 9 8 7 6 5 4

Table Of Contents

April Planner 3
Organize your monthly units, special occasions, and other activities on this form.

April Record Sheet 4
Check out this handy monthly checklist.

Happy Easter! 5
Hop down this bunny trail for some reproducibles that will make Easter extra fun!

Here An Egg, There An Egg… 13
Crack open these ideas for some sunny-side up learning!

Here Come The Babes! 17
Celebrate spring's new arrivals with this cross-curricular unit.

Rain, Rain, Go Away 23
This downpour of reproducibles is just dripping with skills!

"Seed-sations!" 27
It's time to plant some knowledge seedlings in your "kinder-garden"!

It's Earth Day! 33
Teach the importance of taking care of our earth with this clean green unit.

Kindergarten Day 37
Use these "class-y" ideas to celebrate this important part of a child's education.

Bubble Blowout 39
Blow through these reproducibles that are guaranteed to bubble up some excitement.

A Visit To The Pond 43
Invite your little ones to leap amongst these lily pads of learning.

Arbor Day 51
Honor our trees with these "tree-rific" activities.

Just "Brilli-ant"! 53
Set up success in your colony of kindergartners with this buggy unit.

All Through The Town 57
Traveling by land, sea, or air? These on-the-go ideas will get you there!

MEETINGS:

To Do:

Special Dates:

APRIL
Classroom
Themes:

Books To Check Out:

Materials
To Collect:

Duties This
Month:

Birthdays:

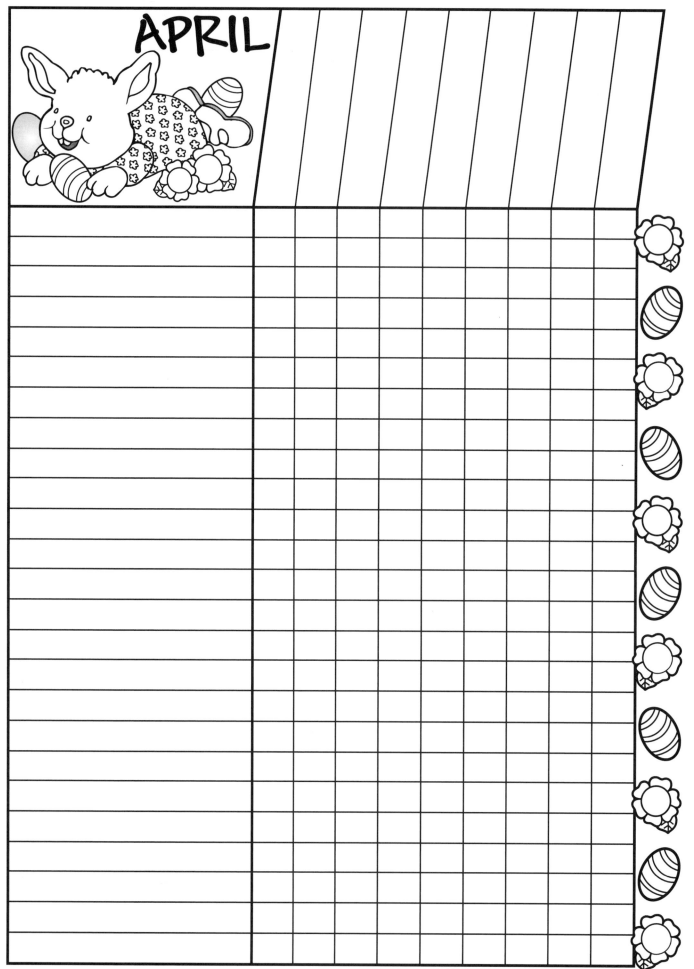

APRIL

Hop down this bunny trail for some "sp-egg-tacular" learning activities to make Easter extra fun!

The Bunny Patch

Delight your children with these programmable bunny manipulatives straight out of the bunny patch! Duplicate a supply of the bunny patterns on page 7 onto pastel-colored tagboard. Cut out the bunnies; then laminate them for reuse. Glue a craft stick onto the back of each bunny card as shown. Use an overhead projection marker to program the bunnies' signs in one of the following ways. To practice another skill, simply wipe the signs with a wet cloth and reprogram.

- Label each of ten bunny cards with a multiple of ten from 10 to 100. Distribute the bunnies to ten students and have them arrange themselves in sequential order.
- Label a class supply of bunny cards with various numerals from 0 to 10. Have each child pick a bunny. Write a basic addition fact on the chalkboard. Encourage students who are holding bunny cards with the correct sum to stand up and hop.
- Use the bunny cards to pair up your students. Label half of the bunnies with uppercase letters and the other half with matching lowercase letters. Invite each child to pick a bunny and find her buddy.

When the bunnies are not in use, store them in this bunny patch. To make the patch, cover the inside of a box lid with mounds of clay. Then spread Easter grass or green shredded tissue paper over the clay. Insert the end of each bunny's stick into the clay. If desired, add a few paper carrot cutouts to the patch. Hippity-hop!

Easter Artists

Invite pairs of students to hop over and practice fine-motor and visual discrimination skills with this artistic game. To prepare, duplicate the gameboard on page 8 onto tagboard and cut it out. Then copy a supply of the bunny outline on page 9 onto white paper. To start the game, each pair of players will need a gameboard, two bunny outlines, two pencils, two game markers (Easter-themed candies work well), and a die. On his turn, a player rolls the die and moves his marker the corresponding number of spaces. He then draws on his bunny outline the feature depicted on the space where his marker has landed. Have the two players continue to roll and draw until they complete their bunnies. To decrease the difficulty for younger students, make one copy of page 9 and use dotted lines to make all of the bunny's features before duplicating the class supply so that your students can trace instead of draw.

5

Mama Hen Counts To Ten

Shoo your little birdies to the math center for this pick-of-the-chick activity. Enlarge the hen-and-chicks math mat on page 10; then color and cut it out. Mount the picture to a piece of tagboard for sturdiness. Cut 20 egg-shaped cards from construction paper. Label each of ten cards with a different numeral from 1 to 10. Label each of the remaining cards with a different number word from *one* to *ten*. Place the picture, the cards, and a dish of jelly beans on a table. Have up to three children at a time work cooperatively to match each numeral to its number word and corresponding set of jelly beans as shown. When the task has been completed, let them fill their little beaks with jelly beans.

What's Missing?

Since Easter usually calls for hunting (colored eggs, that is), and hunting requires a trained eye, there's no better time for this visual discrimination activity. Place five different Easter or spring-related objects in front of your students. Then have each child close his eyes while you remove one of the objects. Encourage the child to open his eyes, study the group, and figure out which object was removed. After several rounds of play, use page 12 as a follow-up activity. Duplicate the page for each child. Have 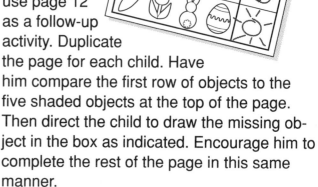 him compare the first row of objects to the five shaded objects at the top of the page. Then direct the child to draw the missing object in the box as indicated. Encourage him to complete the rest of the page in this same manner.

The Easter Egg Stomp

Move over, bunny hop! Here's the newest dance craze, guaranteed to make little tail feathers shake. Duplicate a supply of the egg-shaped movement cards on page 11 onto colored construction paper. Cut out the cards and laminate them if desired. Invite a volunteer to display an appropriate number of cards (depending on the age level of your group) in a pocket chart or along the chalk tray. Slowly "read" through the arrangement and model the sequence of claps and stomps. Encourage the children to join in and repeat this pattern several times. Then have another student change the order of the cards to make a new rhythmic pattern.

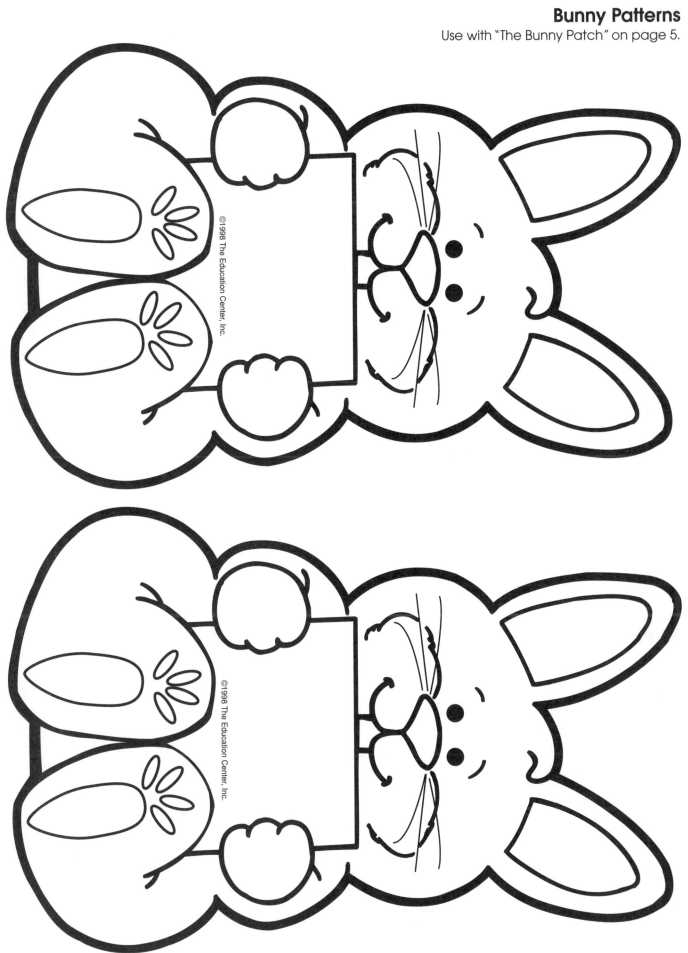

©1998 The Education Center, Inc.

©1998 The Education Center, Inc.

Gameboard
Use with "Easter Artists" on page 5.

head	paws	carrot
eyes	**Easter Artists**	tail
nose	Roll. Move. Draw.	mouth
whiskers	ears	body

Start here.

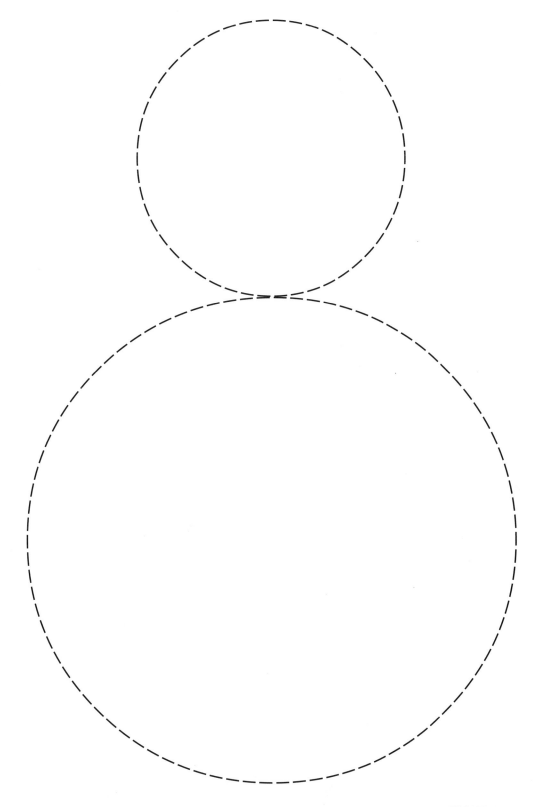

Math Mat

Use with "Mama Hen Counts To Ten" on page 6.

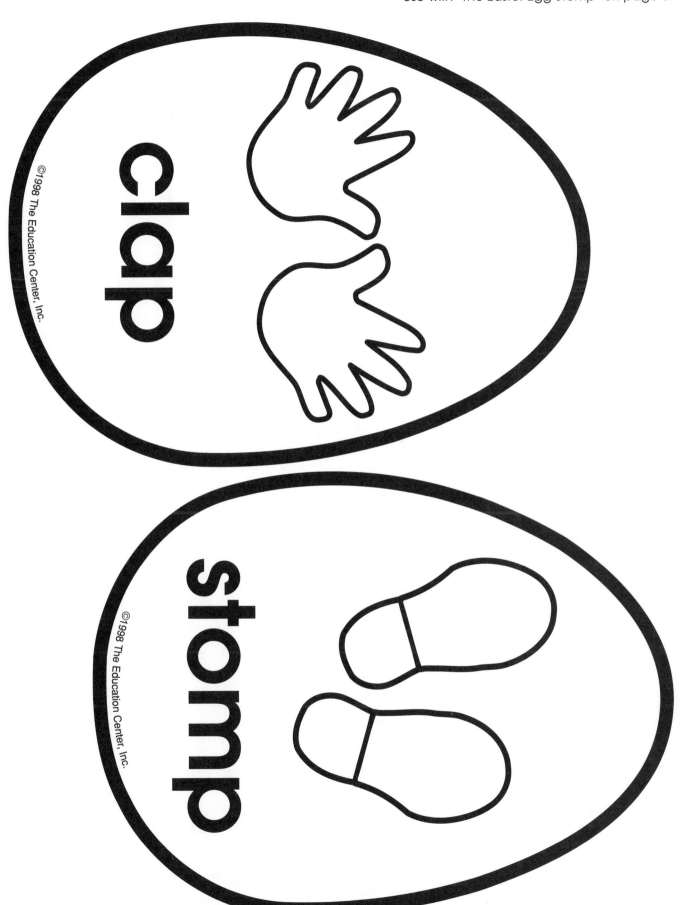

©1998 The Education Center, Inc.

clap

©1998 The Education Center, Inc.

stomp

Name _____

An Easter Hunt

Look at each row.
What is missing?

Draw it.

©1998 The Education Center, Inc. • *April Monthly Reproducibles* • Kindergarten • TEC947

Here An Egg, There An Egg...

Eggs are *everywhere* this time of year. Crack open these activities for some sunny-side up learning fun!

What Is In The Egg?

Hatch an interest in reading with this lift-the-flap booklet filled with basic vocabulary, repetitive text, and picture cues. Duplicate the booklet on pages 14–16 onto white construction paper for each child. Cut each of the pages apart along the dotted line; then give each child a set of the booklet pages. (For ease in construction, lead the group in completing the booklet together, one page at a time.)

To complete the cover, have each child cut around the bold outline and write her name where indicated. Then encourage her to color the egg in any way she chooses. For booklet pages 1 through 4, direct the child to color the animal, cut out the page and pieces, glue the animal to the page as shown, and staple the top of the egg piece to the page so that the animal is hidden. To make the last booklet page, have each child cut out the page and the egg piece, then staple the egg piece to the page as done before. Provide various craft supplies for her to use to decorate the egg for Easter. Then staple a small piece of wrapped candy under the egg flap. (You may choose to do this secretly for an added surprise!) Finish the booklet by having each child stack her pages sequentially behind the cover and then staple them together on the left-hand side. Have your youngsters read the booklet aloud several times; then encourage them to take their booklets home and share them with their families. Congratulations on your new batch of readers!

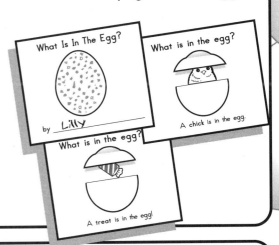

"Egg-stend" The Learning

Use the animals from the "What Is In The Egg?" booklet to practice a basketful of beginning sounds. Label a sentence strip with the beginning sounds *ch, t, d,* and *s* as shown. Place a small toy chick, turtle, duck, and snake in different plastic pull-apart eggs (or use the illustrations from the booklet on pages 14–16). Store the eggs and sentence strip in an Easter basket. As a center activity, have a child crack open each egg and place the animal beside its correct beginning sound on the sentence strip. Increase the difficulty by adding more animals with different beginning sounds. After the task is completed, reward the student with some candy eggs.

Booklet Cover And Page 1

Use with "What Is In The Egg?" on page 13.

What Is In The Egg?

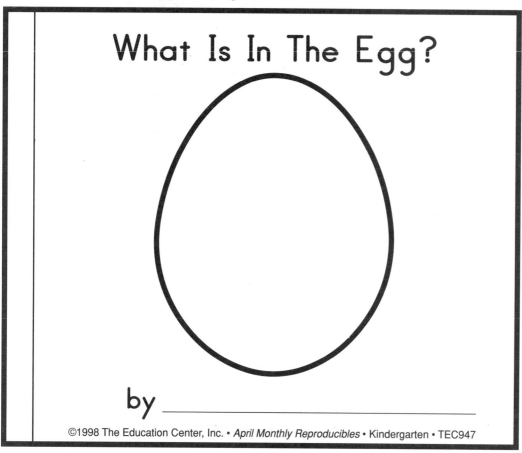

by _____

What is in the egg?

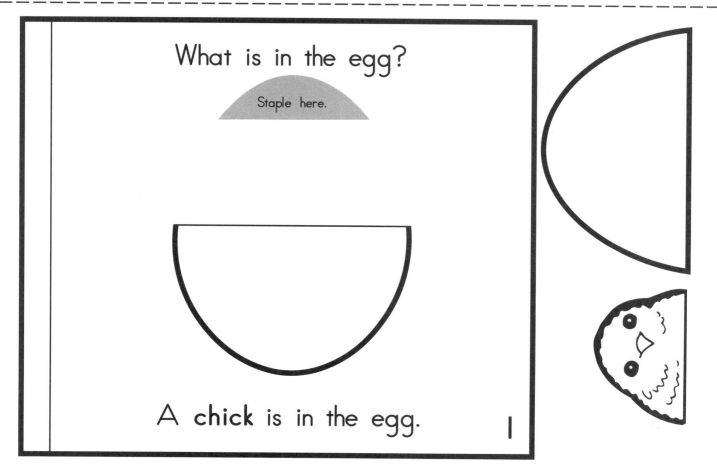

Staple here.

A **chick** is in the egg.

1

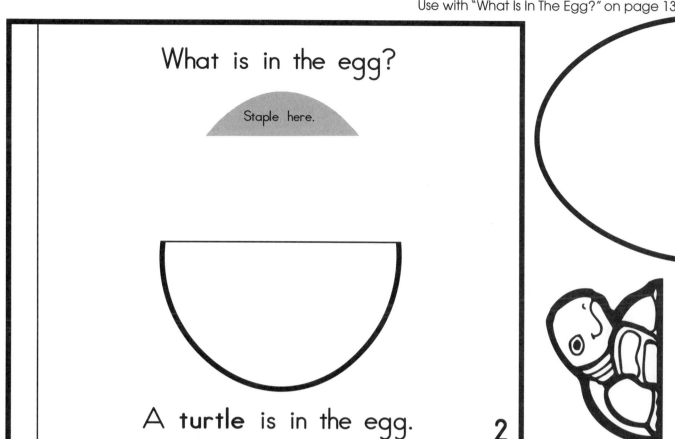

What is in the egg?

Staple here.

A **turtle** is in the egg.

2

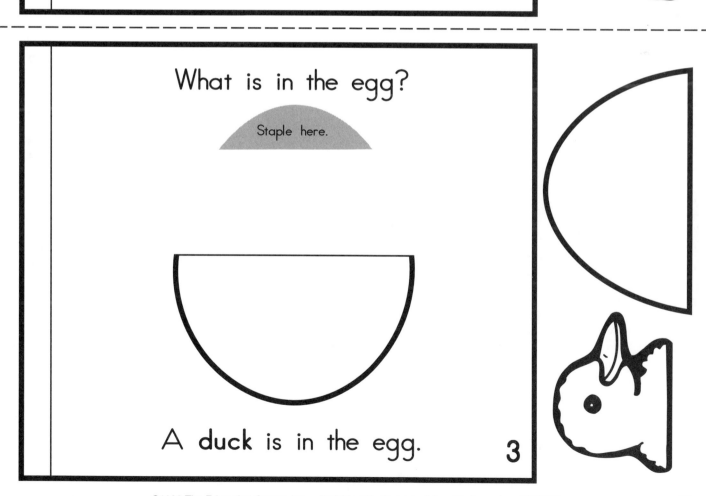

What is in the egg?

Staple here.

A **duck** is in the egg.

3

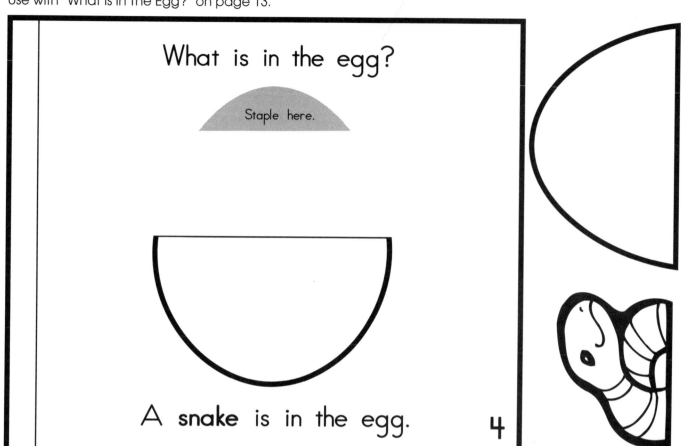

What is in the egg?

Staple here.

A **snake** is in the egg.

4

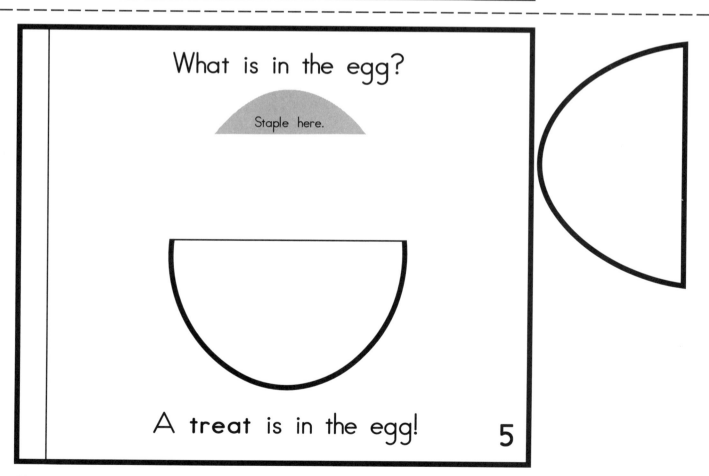

What is in the egg?

Staple here.

A **treat** is in the egg!

5

Here Come The Babes!

Spring is here—that means baby animals are appearing everywhere! Celebrate these new arrivals with the cross-curricular activities found in this unit.

Which Baby Is Next?

Use an assortment of baby animal toys to practice patterning with your youngsters. Form a pattern with several of the animal toys; then have a volunteer come forward and extend the pattern using some of the remaining toys from the assortment. After repeating this several times with different patterns and different volunteers, use the reproducible on page 18 for independent practice.

Barnyard Babies

Your whole class will be chanting "E-I-E-I-O!" after this graphing experience. Give each child ten counters and a copy of page 20. Have students identify the animals represented in the graph at the bottom of the page. Select an animal from the graph and direct each student to place a counter on each of the specified animals he sees in the picture. Then have the youngster count his counters and color the corresponding blocks in the graph. Repeat this procedure for each animal on the graph. Conclude the activity by comparing results and discussing the concepts of *fewest* and *most*.

One Sunny Spring Day

Encourage little ones' creativity with this open-ended rhyming activity. Duplicate page 19 for each child. Brainstorm together several ways to complete the rhyme. Then have each child dictate and illustrate his own idea on his page. If desired, bind the students' work together into a class book for the reading center.

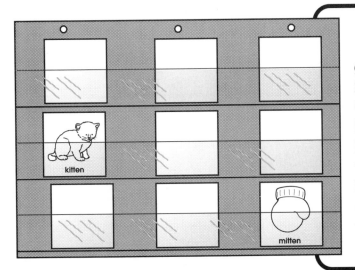

Find The Rhymes

Rhyming words come alive with this fun matching game. Duplicate one copy each of pages 21 and 22 onto white construction paper or tagboard. Color and cut apart the cards. Display the cards in a pocket chart. Invite a student to select a baby animal card. Challenge a different student to find another card that rhymes with the chosen baby's name. Continue until all of the cards are paired. For added difficulty, turn the cards so that the backs are showing in the pocket chart and play a Memory game with them.

Name _____

Which Baby Comes Next?

Cut.

Glue.

©1998 The Education Center, Inc. • *April Monthly Reproducibles* • Kindergarten • TEC947

18

One Sunny Spring Day

As I was playing one sunny spring day,
A baby _____ came _____ my way.

Name _____

Barnyard Babies

How many?
Count.
Graph.

	1	2	3	4	5	6	7	8	9	10
🐷										
🐥										
🐱										
🐮										

calf

laugh

kitten

mitten

cub

tub

chick

stick

fawn

yawn

foal

goal

Rhyming Cards

Use with "Find The Rhymes" on page 17.

kid	lid	lamb
jam	bunny	money
pup	cup	kit
knit	fry	cry

RAIN, RAIN, GO AWAY

April showers have created this downpour of learning activities.
Quick—grab your umbrella! It's raining letters and numbers!

Ducks Like Rain

And so do cats, dogs, and pigs in this activity. Use the reproducible on page 24 as individual reinforcement for ending consonants. As an extension activity, have each child cut out a picture of an animal from a magazine, glue it to the back of her paper, draw an umbrella for it, and label the umbrella with the animal's name or ending sound. Sounds like a splashing good time!

Wet Sets

Although it's nearly impossible to count the raindrops in a passing storm, your youngsters *can* practice their numeration skills with these thunderclouds. Duplicate page 25 for each child. Have her identify the numeral on the first cloud, trace the numeral, and color the corresponding number of raindrops. Encourage the child to complete the rest of the page in this same manner. Kerplink, kerplop, let's count raindrops!

Come Again Another Day

Bring the traditional "Rain, Rain, Go Away" rhyme to life with this nifty craft. Duplicate page 26 onto construction paper for each child. Use an X-acto® knife to slit the window on each pattern along the dotted lines. Have the child color the page; then cut out the pattern and the two strips. Help him tape the strips together where indicated so that the cloud is complete. Then insert the piece through the window and tape the remaining two ends of the strips together to form a loop as shown. Provide paper or fabric scraps for each child to glue around the window to resemble curtains. Finish the project by writing—or asking the child to write—his name in the indicated space on the rhyme. Read the verse aloud several times as you demonstrate how to pull the strip through the window.

23

Name _____

Playing In The Puddles

Say each animal name.
Write the ending sound.

Wet Sets

Trace.
Count.
Color.

9

5

12

8

6

10

Pattern And Strips

Use with "Come Again Another Day" on page 23.

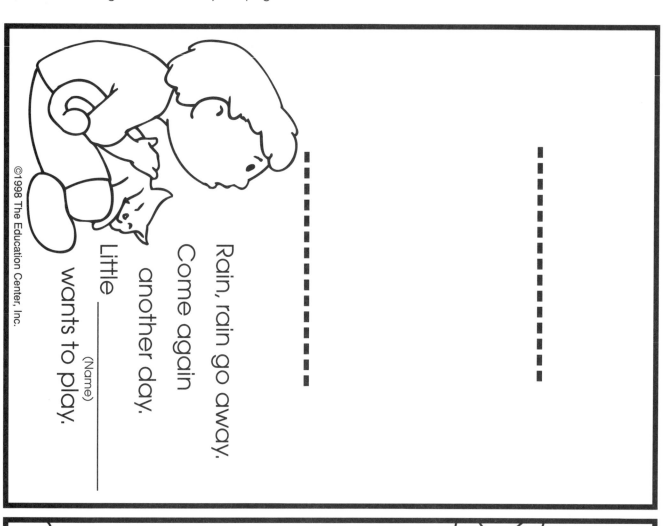

©1998 The Education Center, Inc.

Rain, rain go away.
Come again
another day.
Little _____
(Name)
wants to play.

Overlap here.

Seed-sations!

Pull out your hoe, trowel, and watering can. It's time to plant some knowledge in your "kinder-garden"!

Flannelboard Fun

Does *every* seed grow into a plant? Well, not exactly. Use this flannelboard story to help explain to your little ones the complications a seed may encounter as it tries to grow. Duplicate the patterns on pages 28 and 29 onto construction paper. Then color the patterns, cut them out, and laminate them for durability. Attach felt, sandpaper, or the hook side of a piece of Velcro® to the back of each piece. Then read aloud the following poem while manipulating the pieces as indicated.

Five Little Seeds

Five little seeds blowing in the breeze. *(Place windy cloud and seeds on the board.)*
One little seed gets caught in the trees. *(Cover one seed with the tree.)*

Four little seeds falling to the ground. *(Move the seeds toward the bottom of the board. Place soil under the seeds.)*
A bird eats one that he just found. *(Cover one seed with the bird.)*

Three little seeds getting water and sun. *(Move seeds below soil. Place the rain cloud and sun above the seeds.)*
Two start to grow—but not this one. *(Remove one of the seeds.)*

Two little seeds become little plants. *(Place each plant above the soil aligning it with each seed.)*
One gets stepped on—always that chance! *(Cover one plant with the foot.)*

One little seed made it to full bloom. *(Add bloom to the top of stem.)*
Now new seeds will be traveling soon!

Addition Sprouts

Use the reproducible on page 32 to cultivate students' addition skills. Have each child write the correct sum on each pot, then draw the corresponding number of sprouts in the pot. For added fun, give her a handful of real seeds to use as manipulatives to help solve each equation.

Seed Story Booklet

Now that you've planted the seed's growing dilemma in your students' heads, have them create these individual booklets of the "Five Little Seeds" rhyme to read and share with their families. Duplicate the booklet on pages 30 and 31 for each child. Read through the following directions and gather the necessary materials. Have the child cut the booklet pages apart; then guide him in completing them as described.

Cover: Glue an assortment of seeds to the cover.
Page 1: Color the tree trunk, then sponge-paint the leaves green. Glue a seed onto each X.
Page 2: Glue a seed onto each X. Color the bird, then glue a craft feather on his tail.
Page 3: Glue a seed onto each X. Spread glue under the seeds and sprinkle soil onto the page. Glue gold glitter onto the sun and blue glitter onto the raindrops.
Page 4: Glue a seed onto each X. Color the grass and plants green. Make a fist and dip the pinkie side of your fist into brown paint. Press the painted side of your fist onto one of the plants to make a footprint, as shown. Finish the footprint by making five fingerprinted dots to resemble toes.
Page 5: Glue a seed onto the X. Color the grass and plant green. Repeatedly dip your thumb into yellow paint and make petals at the top of the plant. Glue small seeds to the center of the flower.

When each booklet is completed, place the pages in order behind the cover and staple them along the left side. What a "seed-sational" story!

27

Patterns

Use with "Flannelboard Fun" on page 27.

Five Little Seeds

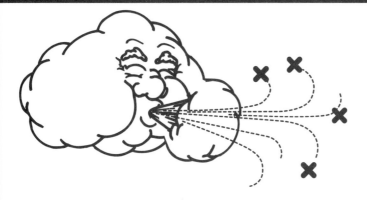

Five little seeds blowing in the breeze.
One little seed gets caught in the trees.

1

Four little seeds falling to the ground.
A bird eats one that he just found.

2

Three little seeds getting water and sun.
Two start to grow—but not this one.

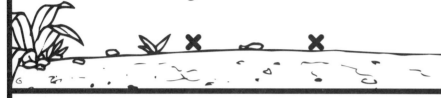

3

Two little seeds become little plants.
One gets stepped on—always that chance!

4

One little seed made it to full bloom.
Now new seeds will be traveling soon!

5

Name _____

 Add.

 Write.

Draw.

Addition Sprouts

2 + 4 =

3 + 4 =

3 + 5 =

2 + 2 =

4 + 6 =

0 + 3 =

2 + 3 =

IT'S EARTH DAY!

Teach the importance of taking care of our earth with these clean green activities.

Put On A Happy Face

Discuss with your youngsters activities that would make the earth smile, such as picking up litter, and those activities that would make the earth frown, such as dumping chemicals into a stream. Challenge each child to do a good deed for the earth sometime during the week, then share her experience with the rest of the group. Use the classification reproducible on page 34 to extend this idea of making the earth happy.

It's In The Bag

Put litter in its place with these Earth Day bags. Collect a class supply of nine-inch paper plates and brown paper grocery bags with handles. Duplicate the poem and title on page 35 for each child. Have the child paint the back of his paper plate blue and green to resemble the earth. Then direct him to color and cut out the poem and title. Instruct the child to glue the poem to one side of the bag and glue the title to the paper plate after the paint dries. To finish each bag, staple the child's paper plate to the opposite side of the bag from the poem. Insert a pair of rubber gloves into each bag, and send your little ones off to save the planet!

Earth-Friendly Snack

Saving the planet is hard work and is sure to build the appetites of your little superheroes. Ease their hunger with the earth-friendly snack on page 36. Be sure to discuss what each ingredient symbolizes as your children construct the treats. Clean air, water, and land sure tastes grand!

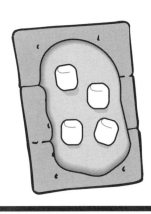

Put On A Happy Face

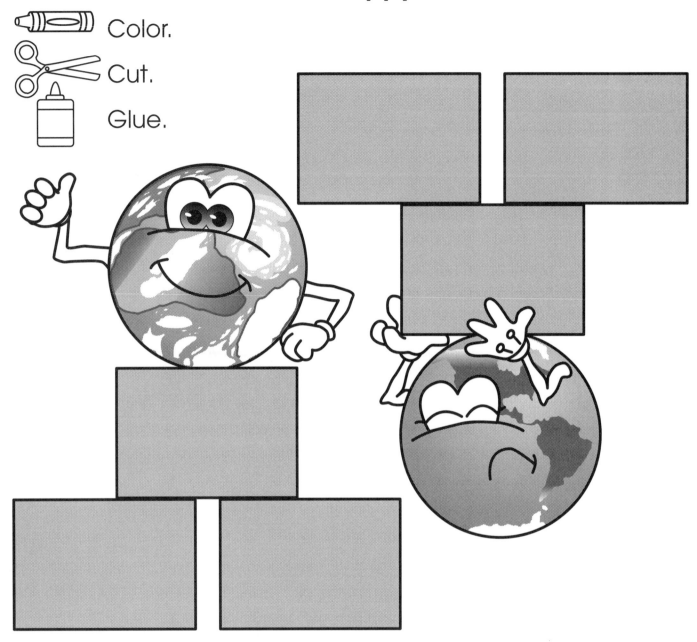

Color.

Cut.

Glue.

In this bag I will place

Lots of litter and some waste.

I want to help our earth stay clean,

And keep nature looking green.

To the world I'd like to say,

"Let's make every day an Earth Day!"

HAPPY EARTH DAY

Name _____

An Earth-Friendly Snack

You will need:

1 napkin

1 plastic knife

1 graham cracker (clean land)

cream cheese tinted blue (clean water)

4 small marshmallows (clean air)

Place the clean land on a napkin.

Spread clean water over the land.

Top the land and water with the clouds of clean air.

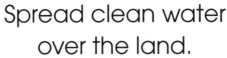

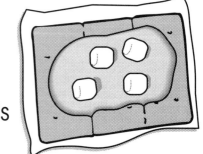

KINDERGARTEN DAY

Can you believe that the first kindergarten was established in 1837? Celebrate this important part of a child's education on April 21 with these "class-y" ideas.

Aa Bb Cc Dd Ee Ff Gg Hh Ii Jj Kk Ll Mm Oo Pp Qq Rr Ss Tt Uu Vv Ww Xx Yy Zz

A Little History

Friedrich Froebel established the very first kindergarten program in Blankenburg, Germany, in 1837. His theories about the importance of music, directed play, and toys to stimulate learning greatly influenced the development of nursery schools in England and the United States. The first American public kindergarten opened its doors in St. Louis, Missouri, in 1873. Froebel's birthdate, April 21, is now also designated as Kindergarten Day.

Dazzling Days

Gather your youngsters together on Kindergarten Day and discuss all of the fun things that have happened over the year. List these experiences on a piece of chart paper. After everyone has had a turn to share a favorite event, add your most memorable moment of the year to the list. My, what a busy year it's been!

Colorful Kindergartners

Use the list made in "Dazzling Days" to create a class book. Duplicate a class supply of page 38 onto various colors of paper. (Or make the copies on white paper and have each child color her page with a color of her choice.) Give each child a page and have her write or dictate an ending to the sentence. Then encourage her to illustrate her page and cut it out.

To make the cover for the book, purchase a yellow file pocket with a Velcro® closure. Use markers or paint to decorate and title the front of the pocket to resemble a crayon box, as shown. Slit the sides of the pocket so that it will open flat. Then use transparent tape to attach each page in a staggered fashion to the inverted portion of the pocket. Close the pocket, secure it with the Velcro® fastener, and it's ready to go! Send the book home with each child so that parents can enjoy the year's highlights. Or use the book during kindergarten registration to ease preschoolers' fears. Kindergarten is a great place to be!

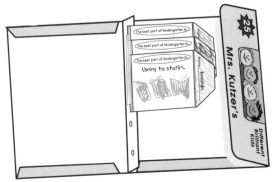

Booklet Page

Use with "Colorful Kindergartners" on page 37.

Name _____

The best part of kindergarten is...

BUBBLE BLOWOUT

Take a deep breath; then blow through the following activities guaranteed to bubble up some excitement and learning fun.

Make-Believe Bubbles

Follow up a reading of *The Bubble Factory* by Tomie dePaola (Grosset & Dunlap) with this imaginative class book. To prepare, duplicate page 40 onto construction paper to make the cover of the book. Then mask out the text on the bubble and make a class supply of page 40 on white paper. Instruct each child to draw a picture of what he would want his magic bubble to turn into. (You may want to have younger students cut out pictures from discarded magazines or catalogs instead of drawing.) Help the child label and personalize his illustration. Then stack these pages behind the cover and staple them together. To finish the book, add glitter around the outlines of the bubbles on the cover. It's magic!

Bubble Bonanza

Bubbles are everywhere in this measurement activity. As your youngsters blow bubbles outdoors, discuss the variety of sizes that are made. Challenge each youngster to pop a small bubble, then a large bubble. Can he find two bubbles that look the same size? After the outdoor exploration, duplicate page 41 for each child and also give him a six-inch length of yarn. Have the child place one end of the yarn on one X of a bubble, then stretch the yarn across the bubble to the other X. Direct him to pinch the yarn to mark the length. Then help him measure the pinched length of yarn with the ruler at the bottom of the page. Have the child record that bubble's diameter in its center, then color the bubble according to the code. Encourage the child to continue measuring the remaining bubbles in this same manner.

"Alpha-Bubbles"

Reviewing the alphabet can be a "pop-ular" activity when you use bubbles. Blow a breath of bubbles; then have a student say a different letter of the alphabet each time he pops a bubble. Challenge him to get as far through the alphabet as possible before the bubbles pop themselves on the ground. As an extension of this activity, have the student name something that begins with whichever letter he said last. Use the reproducible on page 42 as individual reinforcement for recognizing upper- and lowercase letters.

We found some magic bubbles
And thought we'd blow a few.
We dipped the wand into the jar,
And this is what we blew...

Name _____

Bubble Bonanza

Measure across each bubble with yarn.

Write.

Color by the code.

| 1—blue 2—yellow 3—green |

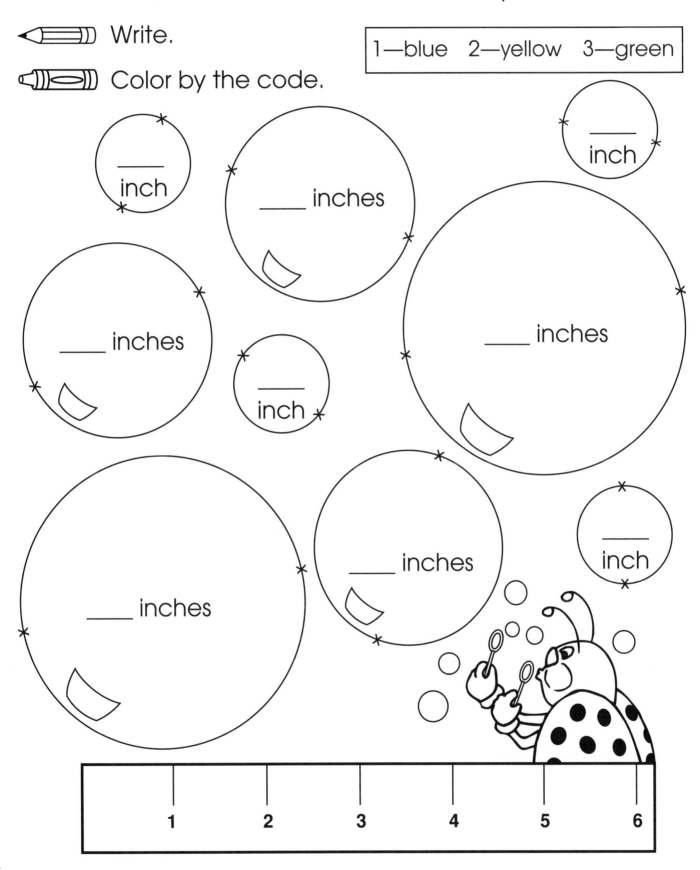

___ inch

___ inches

___ inch

___ inches

___ inch

___ inches

___ inches

___ inches

___ inch

1   2   3   4   5   6

"Alpha-Bubbles"

Find each letter pair.

 Color each pair a different color.

©1998 The Education Center, Inc. • *April Monthly Reproducibles* • Kindergarten • TEC947

Come on down to the pond, where spring is in full bloom! There are lively critters to encounter here as your little ones leap amongst the lily pads of learning.

In The Pond

Make a splash with early readers by inviting youngsters to plunge into this bookmaking activity. Materials needed for each child include six 9" x 12" sheets of white construction paper, six 9-inch paper plates, a hole puncher, one pipe cleaner (cut in half), crayons, blue paint (optional), scissors, glue, and access to a stapler.

To prepare, duplicate pages 45–50 onto the white construction paper for each child. Have the child color or paint her six plates blue. Then stack the plates and punch two holes on the left side. Bind the plates together by inserting a pipe cleaner half through each set of holes and twisting the ends together to form a ring, as shown.

To construct the booklet cover, have each child write her name on the title circle, cut the circle out, and glue it to the center of the first plate. Then direct her to cut out the semicircle pond piece and staple the bottom of it to the bottom of the title circle. Encourage the child to color the cover and decorate with pond life.

To complete the booklet pages, instruct each child to color and cut out the circular pages as you read the text. Then direct her to color, add details to, and cut out the large pattern on each page. (Have her personalize the hair and face on the last page's pattern.) Help the child glue each text page in order to the left side of the book (back of plates), and the corresponding object to the right side of the book, as shown.

An Extra Helping Of Creativity

Want to add more pizzazz to your "In The Pond" booklet pages? Use these alternative suggestions to give the pages a refreshing, "pond-tastic" twist!

Cover: Glue blue glitter around the rim of the plate.

Page 1: Use the fish outline to make a fish-shaped sponge. Brush a thin layer of glue onto the center of the plate. Cover the glue with blue tissue-paper pieces. Sponge-print an orange fish shape on top of the tissue paper. Glue a wiggle eye to the fish.

Page 2: Use the duck outline to cut a duck from yellow felt. Make a crayon-resist water design on the center of the plate with a blue crayon and some blue watercolor. Glue the felt duck to the plate. Glue a yellow craft feather and a wiggle eye onto the duck.

Page 3: Color the center of the plate blue. Color the frog pattern; then cut it out and glue it to the plate. Glue two wiggle eyes to the frog. Glue blue crinkled paper strips around the frog.

Page 4: Use the beaver outline to cut out a beaver from brown construction paper. Draw a nose and mouth with a marker; then glue on a wiggle eye. Paint the center of the plate with light blue paint. Glue the beaver toward the bottom of the painted area. Glue broken pieces of craft sticks and toothpicks above the beaver.

Page 5: Wet the center of the plate with water. Squeeze blue and green food-coloring drops on the wet area. Personalize the hair and face of the child on the pattern; then cut out the pattern and glue it to the plate.

44

Cover Page And Pattern
Use with "In The Pond" on page 43 and
"An Extra Helping Of Creativity" on page 44.

©1998 The Education Center, Inc. • *April Monthly Reproducibles* • *Kindergarten* • *TEC947*

In The Pond

by

_____

Booklet Page 1 And Pattern

Use with "In The Pond" on page 43 and
"An Extra Helping Of Creativity" on page 44.

1

Fish live
in the pond.

Booklet Page 2 And Pattern
Use with "In The Pond" on page 43 and
"An Extra Helping Of Creativity" on page 44.

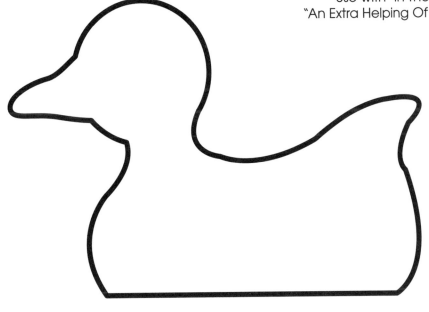

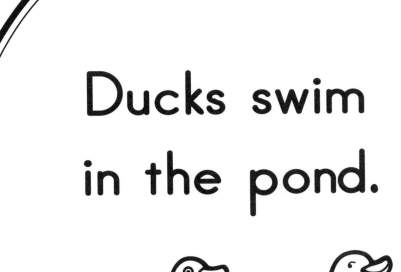

2

Ducks swim
in the pond.

Booklet Page 3 And Pattern
Use with "In The Pond" on page 43 and
"An Extra Helping Of Creativity" on page 44.

Frogs hop
in the pond.

Booklet Page 4 And Pattern
Use with "In The Pond" on page 43 and
"An Extra Helping Of Creativity" on page 44.

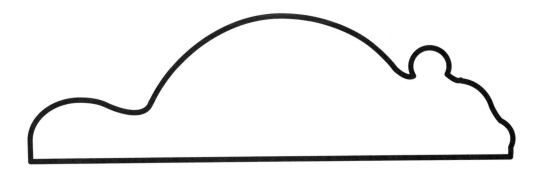

4

Beavers build
in the pond.

Booklet Page 5 And Pattern
Use with "In The Pond" on page 43 and
"An Extra Helping Of Creativity" on page 44.

5

I play
in the pond!

ARBOR DAY

Spend the last Friday in April celebrating Arbor Day with these terrific tree-related activities.

Tried-And-True

That's what trees are! We depend on them for so many things, and they always deliver. Spend some time talking with your youngsters about all that trees do for us. Read aloud an age-appropriate reference book, such as *Be A Friend To Trees* by Patricia Lauber (from the Let's-Read-And-Find-Out Science® series by HarperCollins Publishers, Inc.), to give many examples of trees' good deeds—from providing animal homes to supplying an ingredient in chewing gum. After the reading, challenge your children to recall all of the uses of trees they can remember from the story. Make a list of the responses to use in the bulletin-board activity "Helpful Trees." Trees *are* terrific!

Branch Out With Books

Have You Seen Trees?
By Joanne Oppenheim
Published by Scholastic Inc.

The Apple Pie Tree
By Zoe Hall
Published by The Blue Sky Press

Trees
By Harry Behn
Published by Henry Holt And Company, Inc.

Mary Margaret's Tree
By Blair Drawson
Published by Orchard Books

Sky Tree: Seeing Science Through Art
By Thomas Locker
Published by HarperCollins Publishers, Inc.

MR. BLOCKY'S
BUILDING BLOCKS

60 Blocks
$44.95

Carter

Helpful Trees

Create this "ex-tree" special bulletin-board display with the help of your little ones. To prepare, duplicate the tree pattern on page 52 for each child. Now that your youngsters have learned the many benefits of trees, have each child look through discarded magazines to find an illustration of a tree's use. (Students may refer to their list of tree uses in the activity "Tried-And-True.") Instruct each child to color his tree pattern and write his name on the squirrel's sign. Then direct him to cut out the tree and glue the magazine illustration on it. Display this friendly forest on a bulletin board titled "How 'Wood' Your Tree Help?"

Tree Pattern
Use with "Helpful Trees" on page 51.

Just "Brilli-ant"!

Set up success in your colony of kindergartners with these buggy learning activities.

Do I *Smell* A Picnic?

Or *hear* one? Or *taste* one? Take your youngsters on a snack picnic one day when the weather permits. While they're outside munching, have them name things they see, taste, hear, feel, and smell. Return to the classroom and distribute a copy of page 54 to each child. Have her illustrate each basket with a "sense-ational" picnic memory. Encourage the child to write or dictate a word or phrase for each illustration. Why should the ants have all the fun?

Ants By The Inch

Measurement is a breeze when the ants come marching in! Duplicate a supply of the ant cards on page 56 onto colored construction paper. Cut the cards apart and laminate them for durability. Place 10–12 cards in a resealable plastic bag for each pair of students. Set up several measurement stations, with each station containing multiples of an object. For example, one station might have shoestrings, another station might contain big books, etc. Invite each pair of students to rotate through the stations and use their bag of ant cards to measure the lengths of various items. For a greater challenge, have the pairs of children each find an object in the classroom that measures to a number of cards that you designate.

Ant Farm Charm

Invite your little ones to become worker ants in this beginning-sound discrimination activity. Duplicate page 55 for each child. Read aloud the directions and the name for each of the objects along the bottom of the page. Instruct students to color and cut out the pictures, then glue them to their corresponding chambers. Fantastic!

When I go on a picnic, I...

see _____.

hear _____.

taste _____.

smell _____.

touch _____.

Name _____

Ant Farm Charm

Color.
Cut.
Glue.

Ww

Yy

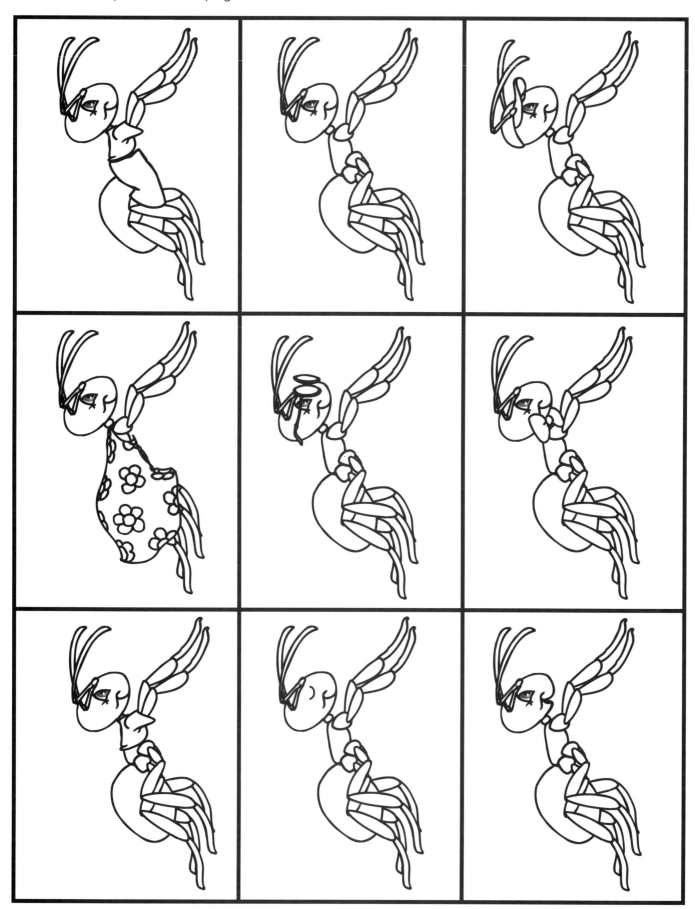

All Through The Town

Whether over the land, across the sea, or through the air—these transportation-themed activities will get you there!

Choo-Choo-Choose A Word

Turn your youngsters into little engineers as they hook up beginning and ending sounds in this whole-group activity. On colorful construction paper, duplicate one train engine and a class supply of boxcars from the patterns on page 59. Cut out the train pieces and laminate them for durability. Designate one child as the engineer. Have him say a word. Write that word on the train engine. Show the engine to the rest of the group and have them name the last sound (or letter) of the word. Then encourage another engineer to say a word that begins with the last sound (or letter) of the previous word. Write this word on a boxcar and display it next to the engine. Continue until everyone has had a turn to climb aboard.

Cruising Down Alphabet Street

This game is sure to rev up young motors as youngsters practice recognizing uppercase and lowercase letter pairs. To prepare, duplicate the gameboard and playing cards on pages 60–62 onto tagboard. Color and cut out the two gameboard pieces; then tape them together and laminate them for durability. If desired, also laminate the cards before cutting them apart. Provide each player with a toy vehicle to use as a game marker. Place the playing cards in a pile facedown where indicated.

To play the game, each player takes a turn picking a card and turning it over. If the letters on the card match, she moves her car forward one space. If the letters are not a pair, the child does not move her car. The game is over when the first player (or all players) reaches the stop sign. Start your engines!

Keep Truckin'

Breaker 1-9, breaker 1-9, all of your kinder-truckers are needed to complete this counting convoy. Duplicate page 63 for each child. Have her cut out each load of freight and glue it onto its corresponding truck. That's a 10-4, good buddy!

Shape Up *And* Ship Out!

Encourage your students to dock these water vessels floating in the harbor. Obtain an even number of toy boats. Use a permanent marker to label the bottom of each pair of vessels with a matching skill of your choice. Place all of the watercraft in your water table. Then invite several students at a time to take turns picking up two of the objects. If they match, remove them from the water. Continue until all of the boats are docked.

"Lotto-motive"

This vehicle lotto game is a great way to culminate your transportation unit. Duplicate page 64 for each child. Then enlarge and cut apart a set of the vehicle pictures from page 64 to use as calling cards. Have the child cut out his lotto playing board. Then direct him to color nine vehicle pictures of his choice, cut them out, and glue them inside different squares on his playing board. Explain that everyone's board needs to be arranged differently, so encourage the child not to copy a neighbor's design. As you call out vehicles in the game, place the corresponding cards in a pocket chart for quick reference. Three in a row—let's go, go, go!

Gameboard

Use with "Cruising Down Alphabet Street" on page 57.

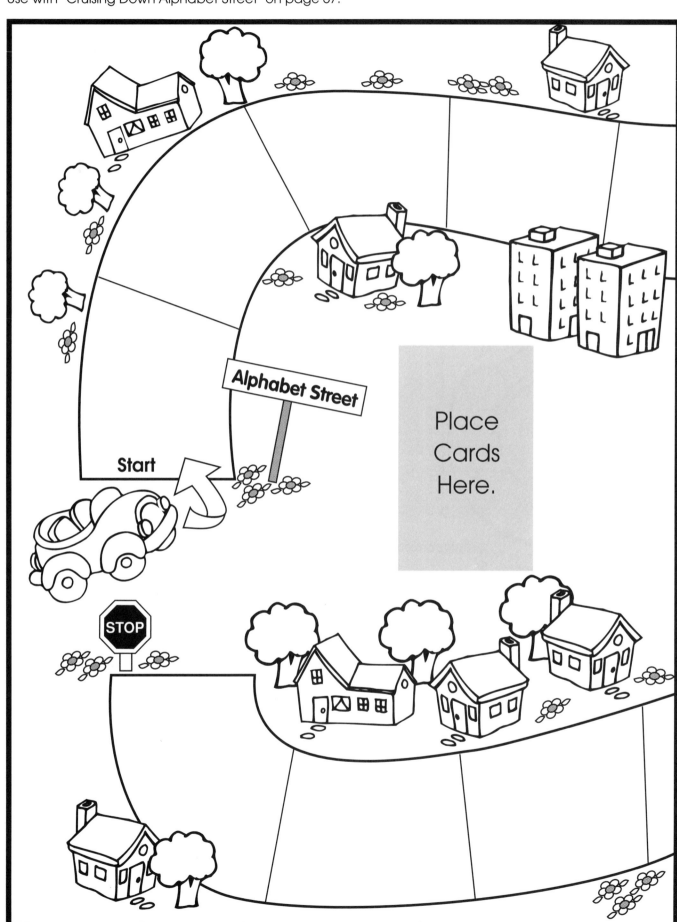

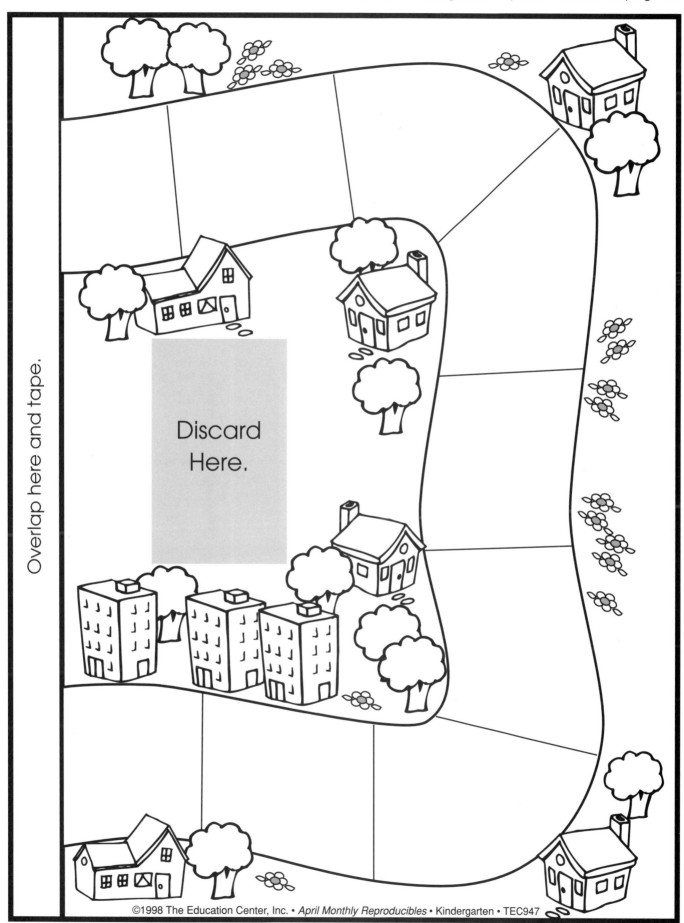

Overlap here and tape.

Discard Here.

A a	C c	G g	H h	K k
M m	O o	R r	T t	Y y
B b	F f	D b	I j	N u
P q	V w	W x	X z	Z s

©1998 The Education Center, Inc. • *April Monthly Reproducibles* • Kindergarten • TEC947

Keep Truckin'

Cut.

Glue.

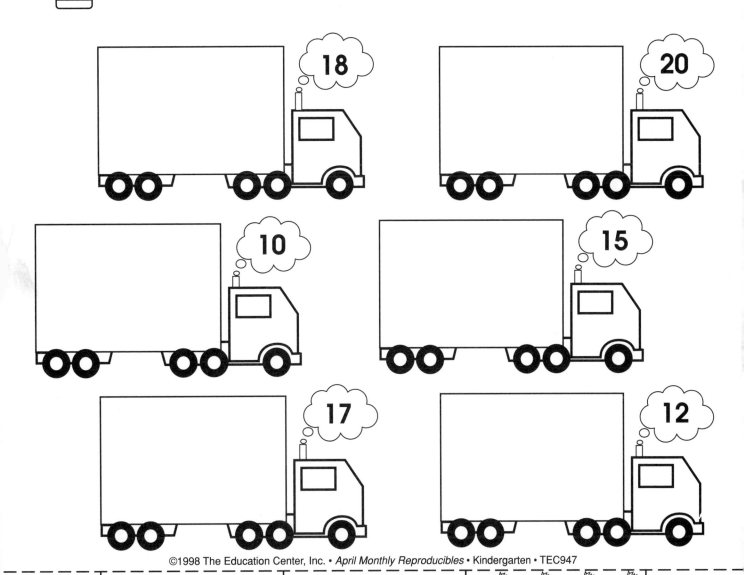

Lotto Game

Use with " 'Lotto-motive' " on page 58.

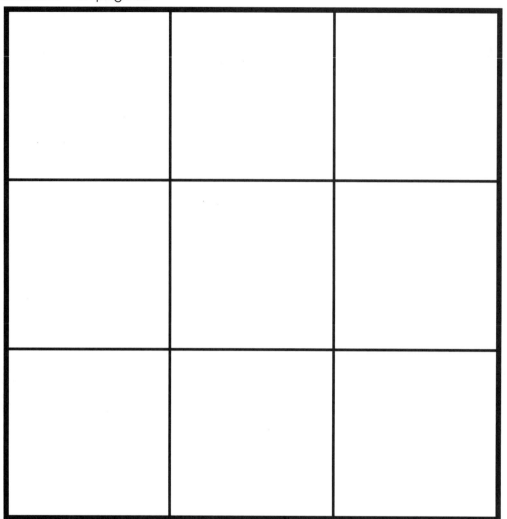